ENIGMAS *of* HISTORY

SEARCHING FOR THE REAL DRACULA

WORLD
BOOK

a Scott Fetzer company

Chicago

www.worldbook.com

World Book edition of "Enigmas de la historia" by Editorial Sol 90.

Enigmas de la historia
Vlad Draculea, el auténtico Drácula

This edition licensed from Editorial Sol 90 S.L.
Copyright 2013 Editorial Sol S.L. All rights reserved.

Revised printing, 2016
English-language revised edition copyright 2015
World Book, Inc.
Enigmas of History
Searching for the Real Dracula

World Book, Inc.
180 North LaSalle Street
Suite 900
Chicago, Illinois 60601 USA

For information about other World Book publications,
visit our website at **www.worldbook.com** or call
1-800-967-5325.

Library of Congress Cataloging-in-Publication Data
Vlad Draculea, el auténtico Drácula. English.
  Searching for the real Dracula. -- English-language
revised edition.
     pages cm. -- (Enigmas of history)
  Originally published as Vlad Draculea, el auténtico
Drácula, Editorial Sol S.L, 2013.
  Summary: "An exploration of the history and legends
  concerning Vlad III (Vlad the Impaler) and his con-
  nection to the folklore and fiction on vampires. Featu-
  res include a map, fact boxes, biographies of authors
  and experts who have written on vampires, places to see
  and visit, a glossary, further readings, and index"--
  Provided by publisher.
  Includes index.
  ISBN 978-0-7166-2674-9
  1. Vlad III, Prince of Wallachia, 1430 or 1431-1476 or
1477--Juvenile literature. 2. Vampires--Folklore--
Juvenile literature. 3. Dracula films--Juvenile literature.
I. World Book, Inc. II. Title. III. Series: Enigmas of
history.
GR830.V3S4313 2015
398.21--dc23
                          2015009313

Enigmas of History Set ISBN: 978-0-7166-2670-1

Printed in China by Shenzhen Donnelley
Printing Co., Ltd., Guangdong Province
2nd printing June 2016

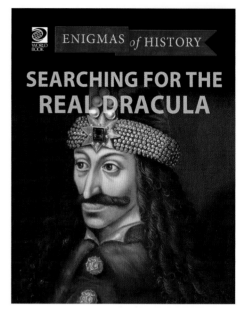

A portrait of Vlad Dracula painted in the 1500's,
which hangs today in Castle Ambras in Innsbruck,
Austria.

© Universal Images Group/SuperStock

Staff

Glossary There is a glossary of terms on page 44. Terms defined in the glossary are in boldface **(type that looks like this)** on their first appearance on any *spread* (two facing pages). Words that are difficult to say are followed by a pronunciation (pruh NUHN see AY shuhn) the first time they are mentioned.

Contents

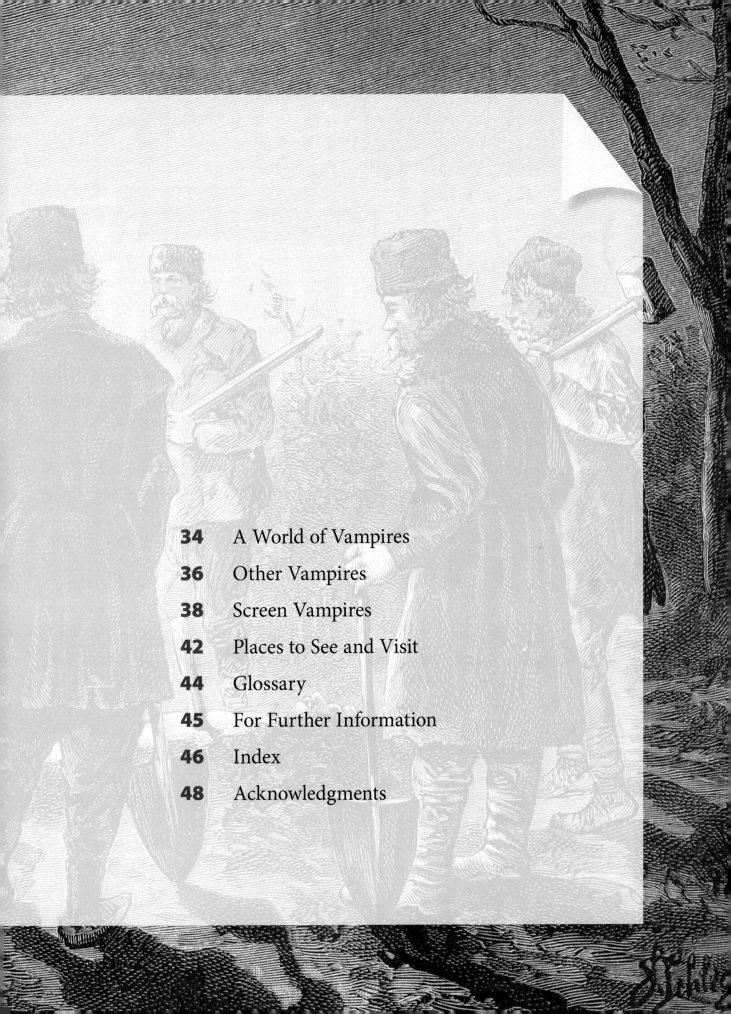

Connecting Count Dracula to Vlad III

Even though much has been written about Vlad Tepes (tsep PESH), or Vlad III, including several biographies, parts of his life remain an *enigma* (a riddle or question). For example, we know he was born in Transylvania (pronounced TRAN sihl VAY nee uh—a region that covers most of present-day central and northwest Romania, in eastern Europe) in the town of Sighisoara (see gee SCHWAR uh). The exact year of his birth is uncertain. He is thought to have been killed during a battle north of the Romanian city of Bucharest (BOO kuh REHST), but the details are unclear. Tradition holds he was buried at Snagov (snah GOVE) Monastery, some 24 miles

(40 kilometers) north of Bucharest (see pages 8-9), although recent historians have suggested other sites.

More information is available, however, about his years in power as **Voivode** (VOY vodh) of Walachia (weh LAY kee uh), especially during the years 1456-1462. But even here there is a problem. The primary sources that provide detail are not reliable. The documents chiefly responsible for shaping the image of Vlad as a merciless **tyrant** (cruel ruler) were a series of pamphlets printed in Germany during the latter decades of the 1400's and distributed throughout Europe. With such unpleasant titles as "The Frightening and Truly Extraordinary Story of a Wicked Bloodthirsty Tyrant

Called Prince Dracula," these accounts offer many stories about Vlad's *atrocities* (very cruel or brutal acts) against not only his enemies but also his own citizens.

Similar tales were recorded by Turkish *chroniclers* (recorders of events) after Vlad's death. Their purpose: to glorify the victory of the **sultan** (Muslim sovereign) over Vlad. A somewhat more fair-minded view was offered in Russian manuscripts which, though acknowledging Vlad's cruelty, supported his desire to establish law and order. Then there are Romanian folk tales, passed from generation to generation for centuries but not written down. These presented Vlad as a **folklore** hero—a man who did what was necessary to maintain the safety and stability of his principality and a leader who stood up to the mighty Turkish army. To this day, Romanians generally regard Vlad as one of their national heroes.

However cruel he may have been, Vlad Tepes was never referred to as a vampire—a corpse that supposedly returns to life at night to suck people's blood—either in historical records or in folk tales. That link was not made until the 1890's, when Irishman Bram Stoker (1847-1912) was writing a vampire novel. Initially, he had intended to name his vampire "Count Wampyr." According to his working notes for *Dracula*, he changed this to "Count Dracula" after finding a short passage in *An Account of the Principalities of Walachia and Moldavia* by William Wilkinson (1820). Wilkinson's text concerned a Walachian voivode named Dracula who fought against the Turks with occasional success. What attracted Stoker to the name was Wilkinson's statement that "*Dracula* in the Walachian language means *devil*." Actually, Vlad's father was known as *Dracul,* which means either *dragon* or *devil. Dracula* means *son of the dragon* or *son of the devil.* Nevertheless, the translation "devil" suited Stoker's purpose well, because he imagined his vampire character as the embodiment of evil. He decided to borrow the name.

Vlad Tepes may be a man of many uncertainties, but one thing is certain: outside of Romania, there would be little interest in Vlad today were it not for the connection between the historical figure and the name given to Bram Stoker's vampire count.

SNAGOV MONASTERY
The body of Vlad III may lie in the
Orthodox *monastery* (a community of
religous men called *monks*) built on
an island in Lake Snagov.

Vlad the Impaler, Son of the Dragon

Vlad the **Impaler** lived in the 1400's. He ruled the principality of Walachia and went down in history for his cruelty, heartless killing, and his natural attraction for spilled blood. In 1897, Bram Stoker used his name for his vampire character, a monstrous drinker of human blood.

Many *civilizations* (societies with complex social, political, and economic institutions) and *cultures* (people with a certain way of life) throughout the world count vampires among their demons. Nearly every culture in the world has some version of a blood-drinking demon or monster. The idea of such demons dates to ancient times.

DRAGON

A figure from the exterior of Vlad Dracula's birthplace.

The Assyrians—a Middle Eastern people who ruled an empire from 800 to 650 B.C.—believed in a demon named Lilitu. A female in form, she drank the blood of small infants. In ancient Greece and Rome, demons called *striges* took the form of birds and preyed on infants by drinking their blood. Ancient stories of blood drinkers are known from Africa, China, India— nearly anywhere stories are told.

Most tales Westerners know of vampires—blood-thirsty, undead predators who feed upon the living— came to us via European stories from the Middle

Ages (400's through 1400's). It was during those dark centuries that vampires ceased to be creatures of legends and stories and, especially in areas of southern Europe, became creatures in the local graveyard to be feared. People in Europe in the Middle Ages, especially small farming communities, began to seriously believe in and fear the evil that the dead could do them should the dead rise from their graves.

Apostates (people who give up the religion into which they were born), the *excommunicated* (people cut off from membership in their church), suicide or murder victims, or criminals and evil people who had gravely trespassed God's laws and died in sin, all were believed to become servants of the devil in their **afterlife.** These undead were thought to be capable of causing death in the community via illnesses and *epidemics* (outbreaks of disease in many people at about the same time). The church took advantage of such fears, presenting itself as a shield against these embodiments of Evil.

Superstition (an unreasoning fear of what is unknown, mysterious, or imaginary, especially in connection with religion) and fantasy seemed to become reality in the mid-1400's. Courts in France condemned the nobleman Gilles de Rais, at one time an officer in the Hundred Years' War (1337-1453), to death by hanging for murdering scores of children. Rais was also charged and found guilty of attempting to summon demons. About 40 years after

COLD AS ICE

The image of Vlad Tepes, captured in an oil painting from the 1500's that hangs in a palace in Austria. Tepes was not a last name for Vlad III, but a title, meaning *the Impaler*. To *impale* is to torture and kill someone by thrusting them upon a pointed stake.

the trial and execution of Rais, the attitude of the Roman Catholic Church regarding witchcraft changed. Faced with an increase in the number of cases of witchcraft and devil worship, Pope Innocent VIII (1432-1492) published in 1484 the papal *bull* (decree) "Summis desiderantes affectibus." In this publication, the Church recognized the dangers of witchcraft after 500 years of denying its existence. Two years later, two German priests published *Malleus Maleficarum (Hammer of the Witches)*, which detailed how to identify and punish witches. Strangely, in an attempt to combat the danger of evil, the priests put a human face on the **superstition** that demons live among mortals.

At the beginning of the 1600's, the Hungarian Countess Elizabeth Báthory proved this idea by being suspected of vampirism. It is reported that in an effort to preserve the youthfulness of her skin, the countess ordered the murder of more than 600 young people, in whose fresh blood she would periodically bathe. In this same era, the fear of vampires reached new heights in central Europe and the Balkans.

TIME OF THE VAMPIRES

These superstitions strengthened in following centuries and were officially documented. Two Serbian farmers, Peter Plogojovitz and Arnold Paole, became well-known in 1725 and 1732 when they reportedly rose from their graves, caused the deaths of several people, and lengthened epidemics. At the same time, "scientific" literature about vampirism appeared and reached its height with the lengthy work of Augustin Calmet, *Dissertations sur les Apparitions des Anges, des Démons & des Esprits et sur les Revenants et Vampires de Hongrie, de Bohême, de Moravie & de Silésie* (Dissertations upon the Apparitions of Angels,

Demons, and Ghosts, and Concerning the Vampires of Hungary, Bohemia, Moravia, and Silesia), in which the French abbot confirmed that Hungary had the largest number of cases of vampirism recorded in Central Europe and the Balkans. Faced with this renewed wave of popular superstition surrounding blood drinkers, even the beloved Pope Benedict XIV (1675-1758) published, in 1749, the pamphlet "Vampires in the Light of Science," in an effort to show that these evil beings did not exist.

Despite the spread of the vampire myth throughout nearly all of Europe, by the 1800's, new ideas caused by the increase of scientific

thinking and knowledge turned this myth back into the **folklore** it was. Still, these tales lived on as truth in some remote corners of Central Europe and Asia, where a mixture of ethnic groups and beliefs allowed it to survive.

Romanticism (a style in the fine arts and literature that emphasizes imagination and intuition rather than logic) and the short story *The Vampyre* (1816) by Doctor John Polidori, inspired by the British poet Lord Byron (1788-1824), revived the myth. It converted it into a product of literary imagination, making vampires the main characters of terrifying **gothic** novels and serials, types of books that enjoyed great

success among readers in the late 1700's and 1800's.

In 1897, an Irish novelist, Bram Stoker, published *Dracula*, the terrifying tale of an aristocratic vampire. This Transylvanian count possesses supernatural powers and keeps or recovers his health at the expense of a group of British friends.

In writing the book, the author was inspired by the works of other writers, such as *Carmilla* (1872) by the Irish author Sheridan Le Fanu, (1814-1873). Stoker thoroughly researched the remote Hungarian region of Transylvania, where the fear of vampires had continued for centuries. During his research, Stoker made the acquaintance of a

Hungarian language expert who may have given Stoker the name of his vampire: Dracula. The scholar recounted the bloody history of Vlad the Impaler, a prince of Walachia in the mid-1400's who was known for his cruelty. Vlad's last name was Dracula, which, in Romanian, the Walachian tongue, means both *Son of the Dragon* and *Son of the Devil*. The suggestive meaning must have delighted Stoker, who not only honored his Hungarian collaborator in a passage of his novel, but also made famous Vlad the Impaler, whose terrible deeds terrified Europe in the 1400's, when German pamphlets presented him as a blood-thirsty tyrant.

THE TURKISH THREAT

The Hungarian King Sigismund (riding the white horse in the illustration, above left) created the Order of the Dragon to fight the Turkish threat in Eastern Europe.

POENARI CASTLE

Overlooking the Arges River in Walachia, this inaccessible castle (above) was the true home of Vlad III Dracula, rather than the Transylvanian castle of Bran.

THE TRUE DRACULA

Vlad Dracula was born in Schässburg (now Sighisoara), a Saxon city in Transylvania, in around 1431. His father was Vlad II Dracul, son of Mircea (meer chuh) the Elder, who guided Walachia to its golden age. Walachia extended from the Carpathian Mountains to the Danube River in the mid-1400's.

At the time Vlad III was born, Walachia was in the middle of a power struggle between the Ottoman Empire and the Kingdom of Hungary. The Ottomans, who were **nomadic** Turkish peoples, had conquered much of southeastern Europe by the late 1300's. The Walachian principality depended for its existence on diplomacy and the **tribute** (money paid by one nation to another for peace or protection) paid to its powerful Ottoman neighbors. The principality was a buffer between the Turks (the Ottomans) and the Hungarians.

Because one could easily access Hungary's rich industrial region of Transylvania from Walachia, the royal court at Buda always showed great interest in who occupied the throne of the smaller kingdom.

In light of this interest, it makes sense that Sigismund, the King of Hungary, would give to Vlad III's father the title of Knight of the Order of the Dragon. To honor this title, Vlad II adopted the last name Dracul, which means *dragon* in Romanian. The order was established in the struggle against the Turks, and Vlad II was offered a position as **Voivode** of Transylvania in 1431.

This interest in Walachian affairs could work both ways, however. In 1447, John Hunyadi, the Hungarian regent, ordered that Vlad II Dracul be taken off the throne and executed. Being unable to count on Hungary's protection, Vlad II gave in to a request from the Turkish **sultan** concerning his sons.

TURKISH HOSTAGES

Vlad II's sons, Vlad and Radu, were sent to the Turkish court as hostages when the younger Vlad was only eight years old. The boys were educated in the military arts and knew Mehmet II (1432-1481), also spelled Mehmed II, who was the seventh sultan of the Ottoman Empire. Mehmet II conquered Constantinople (now Istanbul), the capital of the Byzantine Empire (which at that time covered parts of what is now Turkey and Greece) early in his reign.

During the nine years Vlad lived among the Ottomans, he observed the power of their empire. Its organization was very different from the feudal Hungarian model. In a **feudal system,** people, usually farmers, gave military and other services to a lord in return for his protection and the use of his land. In contrast, the Ottoman Empire was centered on the authority of the sultan and was protected by the best organized army in Europe.

Because of the instability of the Walachian princedom and political shifts in Hungary and the Ottoman Empire, Vlad III Dracula was named voivode on three separate occasions. During his second and longest reign, from 1456 to 1462, he acted as a Renaissance prince, preoccupied with concentrating power for himself. To do this, he reportedly did not hesitate to use terror and extreme violence to encourage loyalty. As an example, after taking revenge for the deaths of his father and older brother by executing the voivode responsible and impaling the **boyars** (nobles) who betrayed them, he did the same to the people who lived in the Transylvanian cities of Kronstadt and Hermannstadt, who had opposed him, and to the Turkish prisoners captured. Historians, influenced by German accounts, considered him a bloodthirsty monster.

Bram Stoker (1847-1912)

Stories of terror and mystery were a part of Abraham (Bram) Stoker's life from infancy. Bedridden until eight years of age, his mother told him frightening tales and legends about the Great Famine of Ireland. As a member of the Protestant minority in Dublin, he received an elite education at Trinity College, where he shone in literature and mathematics and came to love the theater. He was a friend of Irish poet and playwright Oscar Wilde (1854-1900). In 1876, the famous British actor Henry Irving (1838-1905) hired Stoker as the manager and secretary of his company, a position he retained until the actor's death. This position allowed him to travel the world, and he became a member of the secret society "Golden Dawn," a group devoted to mysticism (the belief that God or spiritual truths can be known through individual insight, rather than by reasoning or study). Attracted by the mystery, he began writing *Dracula* in 1890, though he originally titled it *The Undead.*

DRACULA Stoker gave this most celebrated of vampires a link to the historic figure of Vlad III, and gave a surprising veracity to the novel itself through the use of the *epistolary genre* (written in the form of a series of letters).

> *"There are mysteries which men can only guess at, which age by age they may solve only in part."* Bram Stoker (in *Dracula*).

Timothy Taylor

(1960-)

This British **archaeologist** uses his scientific knowledge to study burial practices among Europeans. His book *The Buried Soul: How Humans Invented Death* (2004) has extensive information on burial practices that indicate that people believed in and took actions to guard against vampirism in many parts of Europe during the Middle Ages (400-1400).

SCIENTIST Taylor has excavated grave sites to study the burial practices of Europeans.

Dom Augustin Calmet (1672-1757)

Born in the Lorraine region of north-eastern France, this Benedictine *abbot* (head of a monastery) was a well-known scholar. He is best known for his inter-pretations of the Bible and his knowledge of theology, archaeology, and history of the Hebrew people. He acquired fame without meaning to when, in 1746, he published a collection of documented cases of vampirism in Central Europe: *Dissertations Upon the Apparitions of Angels, Demons, and Ghosts. and Concerning the Vampires of Hungary, Bohemia, Moravia, and Silesia.* The work received a warm welcome, and the abbot accidentally contributed to reviving interest in vampires and the dark arts.

FOUNDER Calmet is considered the founder of vampirology, as his erudite knowledge gave the vampire mystery a "scientific" basis.

Dracula's Territory

In the 1400's, Walachia was divided by conflicts between **dynasties** (ruling families). Its existence depended on its princes' diplomatic ability to please its powerful neighbors, Hungary and the Ottoman Empire. Vlad III worked to create a powerful, independent state using terror, but failed in the end.

Powerful Contemporaries

Vlad III reigned at the same time as other strong rulers who favored *absolute monarchy* (monarchy in which there is no restriction of the ruler's political power). At times, Vlad III formed treaties with these other monarchs; sometimes he was in conflict with them.

Mehmet II, the Conqueror (1432-1481)

The third son of Murad II, he became the **sultan** in 1444. Known as the conqueror of Constantinople (in 1453), he was a model absolute monarch among his contemporaries and expanded the Ottoman Empire into the Balkans, Asia Minor, and Crimea. Mehmet II and Vlad III Dracula met as adolescents in the city of Edirne in Turkey.

Stefan the Great (1433-1504)

The Prince of Moldova, he was Vlad III's cousin on his mother's side. Thanks to the military support of his Walachian relative, Stefan took the throne in 1457. He was a pious, modern prince and a lover of culture. He gathered an army strong enough to stop the ambitions of the Ottomans, Hungarians, and Polish. He challenged Radu the Handsome, his cousin and Vlad's brother, and Basarab III the Old during the period in which Walachia was under Turkish rule.

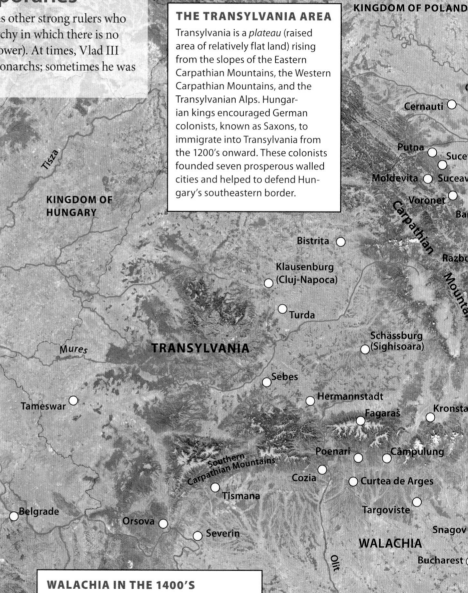

THE TRANSYLVANIA AREA

Transylvania is a *plateau* (raised area of relatively flat land) rising from the slopes of the Eastern Carpathian Mountains, the Western Carpathian Mountains, and the Transylvanian Alps. Hungarian kings encouraged German colonists, known as Saxons, to immigrate into Transylvania from the 1200's onward. These colonists founded seven prosperous walled cities and helped to defend Hungary's southeastern border.

WALACHIA IN THE 1400'S

Walachia occupied a plain that extended from the southern Carpathian Mountains to the waters of the Danube, and from the Siret River, to the east, to the narrow confines of the Danube gorge known as the Iron Gates, to the west. Half a million Walachians inhabited the principality. Cities were small and poorly defended.

KINGDOM OF POLAND

Cernauti

Putna
Suce
Moldevita Suceav
Voronet
Ba

KINGDOM OF HUNGARY

Tisza

Bistrita

Klausenburg (Cluj-Napoca)

Razbo

Turda

Carpathian Mounta

Schässburg (Sighisoara)

Mures

TRANSYLVANIA

Sebes

Hermannstadt

Tameswar

Fagaraš Kronsta

Poenari Câmpulung

Southern Carpathian Mountains

Cozia Curtea de Arges

Tismana

Targoviste

Belgrade

Orsova

Severin

Snagov

WALACHIA

Olit

Bucharest

Giurgiu

Danube Nicopolis Rousse

OTTOMAN EMPIRE

Was the Walachian Prince Born in a Saxon City in Transylvania?

Prince Vlad III's birthplace remains a mystery. Most historians believe that he was born in the Saxon city of Schässburg (now Sighisoara), in Transylvania, while his father was in exile. Others believe he was born in Targoviste, the Walachian capital, shortly after Alexander Aldea, his father's stepbrother, took the throne.

EASTERN EUROPE, 1450

Baltic Sea

TEUTONIC ORDER

• Minsk

RUSSIAN PRINCIPALITIES

HOLY ROMAN EMPIRE

• Warsaw

LITHUANIA

KHANATE OF THE GOLDEN HORDE

KINGDOM OF POLAND

Nuremberg
• BOHEMIA

• Krakow

• Kiev

• Munich • Vienna

• Buda

MOLDAVIA

• Astrakhan

KINGDOM OF HUNGARY

VENICE • Ljubljana

Belgrade

• Targoviste

Caspian Sea

BOSNIA

WALACHIA

• Kaffa

• Florence

SERBIA

• Sofia

Black Sea

GEORGIA

• Rome

OTTOMAN EMPIRE

Constantinople

KINGDOM OF THE TWO SICILIES

ALBANIA

• Ankara

CARAMANIA

ATHENS

RAMASAN

Mediterranean Sea

CRETE —

CYPRUS —

MAMLUK SULTANATE

Dniester

enez

Pruth

MOLDOVA

Iasi ○

Chisinau ○

Siret

Vaslui ○

Akkerman ○

BLACK SEA

Galat ○

Chilia ○

Braila ○

Isaccea ○

Silistra ○

kan

ENEMY AND ALLY

John Hunyadi (?-1456), the "Vanquisher of Turks"
A noble of Walachian origin, he was the Count of Severin, **Voivode** of Transylvania, Captain General of Belgrade, and Regent of Hungary from 1446 to 1453. Confronted by Vlad Dracula, whom he considered a weak but cunning ally for cooperating with the Turks after the open crisis in Hungary caused by the death of King Albert II (ruled 1437-1439), Hunyadi initiated the 1447 military offensive against Walachia. The offensive resulted in the deaths of Vlad III's father and brother.

Chindia Tower (photo) in the royal complex at Targoviste and the oldest stretch of the walls of Bucharest were commissioned by Vlad III, who converted the modest village into a well-fortified city.

Matthias Corvinus (1443-1490)
The second son of John Hunyadi, he was elected king of Hungary in 1458. He created a permanent army, making Hungary a large empire. In the conflicts within the nobility that followed the deaths of John Hunyadi and Ladislaus V the Posthumous, Vlad III Dracula was a firm ally of Michael Szilagyi, Matthias's uncle.

Different Neighbors

Despite their religious differences, the Walachian and Transylvanian societies were economically compatible and shared the same fear of Ottoman oppression. The people of Walachia came from similar backgrounds. Transylvanians were from a mix of backgrounds. They generally enjoyed more privileges than the Walachians.

The Classes of the Walachian Principality

The people of Walachia, known as Walachians, spoke Romanian, a language that came from the Latin language. Walachians were Orthodox Christian in faith, and their main source of livelihood was livestock. The **voivode** was the most important person in Walachian society, followed by the **boyars** and the *clergy* (priests and monks). Farmers were found at the bottom of this *hierarchy* (organizational ranks).

Boyars
With a name of Slavic origin, they made up the Walachian nobility. Landowners, they rented their lands to free farmers or forced their **serfs** (peasants) to work the land. They supplied military forces in the event of armed conflict.

Clergy
Orthodox clergy lived mostly in monasteries and had their own lands. They were independent of the church in Rome, which helped to give the Walachian state legal standing.

Serfs
They depended on their masters. They were poor farmers who worked for the boyars or monasteries. Only slaves were beneath them in status.

Farmers
Free farmers could own land or provide their services to the boyars. In exchange for this privilege, they served in the military when called for by the voivode.

Roma
The first written indication of the presence of Roma in Walachia was in 1385. At first, these Asian **nomads** offered their knowledge and services to landowners, but from the 1400's onward, they were considered to be of the same status as slaves.

The Prince
The voivode was elected by an assembly of boyars and the clergy. There was no right of succession by birth to the throne in Walachia, and kings were elected or chosen from the current sovereign's descendants.

Walled Churches

On Hungary's eastern frontier, Transylvania's landscape was noted for its walled cities. Imitating the military architecture of the Teutonic Knights (a group of German crusaders from the 1100's) and trusting in the protection of God, Saxon colonists built walled churches in the countryside, which then became a refuge when the colonists were faced with foreign attacks.

The Complex Transylvanian Society

Though there were governmental differences between Walachia and Transylvania, the most important difference was Transylvania's many ethnic groups, vastly different than Walachia's uniform culture. Hungarians, Szeklers, Saxons, and Walachians coexisted in this dependency of Hungary found at the foot of the Carpathian Mountains. Excepting the Walachians, the inhabitants of Transylvania were Roman Catholics.

Szeklers

Szeklers were a *Magyar* (Hungarian) military class assigned to guard the frontiers of southeastern Transylvania by the Hungarian king. On par with the Hungarian nobility, they owed allegiance only to the prince.

Hungarians
Hungarian nobility were the dominant social class. The Hungarian king usually selected the Transylvanian voivode from among his followers. They had large agricultural properties and exploited the serfs.

Saxons
These people were descendants of the German immigrants from the 1100's and 1200's who founded cities in northern and southern Transylvania. They were *artisans* (skilled workers) and controlled most businesses. They also enjoyed great privileges.

Walachians
Walachians were one of the largest population groups in Transylvania. Attracted by the Hungarian kings, they settled in northern Transylvania in the 1200's. They lacked privileges and fell into servitude over time.

The Court at Targoviste

At the end of the 1300's, Mircea the Elder decided to move the capital of Walachia from Curtea de Arges to Targoviste, where the royal court resided. Some of the best known and most violent episodes in Vlad Dracula's life took place here.

1 SAINT FRIDAY CHURCH
This is the only church in Romania that retains the characteristics of religious architecture from the 1400's. Also known as the "small church," it was the first church on the royal premises.

2 ROYAL PALACE

Mircea the Elder started constructing dwelling for the royal family in the 1300's. The ruins tod contain the remains of the expansion performe over the course of the 1400's.

Birthplace of Vlad III

Most believe that Vlad Dracula was born far from Targoviste, in a home owned by Vlad Dracul in the city of Sighisoara, in Transylvania. Vlad Dracula was the eldest son born of Vlad Dracul's second marriage. Vlad II Dracul was the son of Mircea the Elder, and had just been named a knight in the Order of the Dragon and **Voivode** of Transylvania by King Sigismund of Hungary.

Was Vlad Dracula a Vampire?

Converted into a legend, the "Son of the Dragon" was also known as the "Son of the Devil" and came to represent absolute evil. However, he was not identified with vampires until much later, in the 1800's.

German and Hungarian legends from the 1500's describe Vlad III as uncivilized and a **tyrant,** but they gave him none of the characteristics of a vampire. It was not until the 1897 publication of the novel *Dracula* in London by Irishman Bram Stoker that Vlad began to be associated with vampires. This was primarily due to the power of his name. Vlad Dracula was not just the "Son of the Dragon." In Romanian, *drac* also means "devil." That is, Dracula is also the "Son of the Devil." Thus a single word has two meanings, devil and dragon, the second a mythological animal that is synonymous with evil in Christian tradition.

STOKER AND VLAD III

Carmilla, a vampire story published in 1872 by Sheridan Le Fanu, had captured Stoker's attention, as had the notable work by Scottish anthropologist Sir James Frazer, *The Golden Bough,* published in 1890, which recounts the vampiric traditions of Transylvania. But there was more.

Stoker also took note of Emily Gerard's work *Transylvanian Superstitions*, which touched on vampires. In the Whitby public library, Stoker found *An Account of the Principalities of Walachia and Moldavia,* a report by William Wilkinson published in 1820 that dedicated a brief paragraph to a prince of the 1400's named Dracula. Stoker not only took note of this paragraph, but also took the name "Dracula" for the villain in the vampire novel he had begun to write. Some researchers suggest that Stoker learned much more about Vlad the Impaler in an 1890 meeting with Hungarian scholar Arminius Vámbéry, whose *History of Hungary* had been published in London in 1887. Although they did meet, there is no proof that Vámbéry talked about Vlad. There is also no evidence that Stoker researched Vlad the Impaler in the British Museum, which holds information about Vlad III, including a German pamphlet from the 1400's portraying the prince eating among numerous impaled victims while one of his servants cuts apart human bodies with an axe.

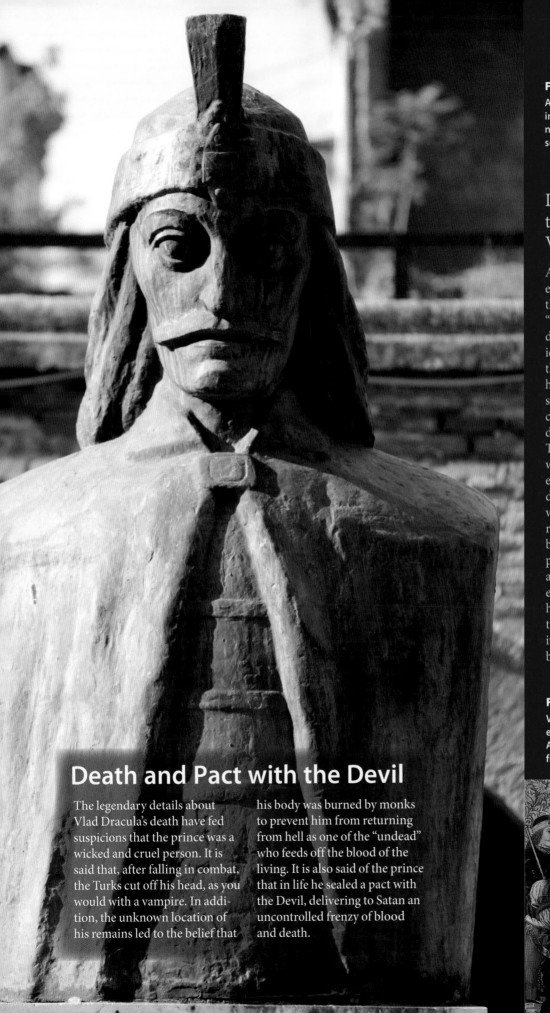

Did Vlad III Drink the Blood of His Victims?

According to the black legend surrounding Vlad III that describes him as a "blood-thirsty demon," as he dined beneath impaled bodies, he dipped his bread in the blood flowing down the hideous spikes, while his servants collected blood in a cup from which the prince drank with great enjoyment. The Voivode of Walachia was certainly the cruel leader of a small, unstable kingdom. Conscious of this weakness, Vlad the Impaler resorted to extremely cruel, bloody methods for the purpose of sowing terror among his underlings and enemies, but there is no historical record showing that the prince's dietary habits included drinking human blood.

Death and Pact with the Devil

The legendary details about Vlad Dracula's death have fed suspicions that the prince was a wicked and cruel person. It is said that, after falling in combat, the Turks cut off his head, as you would with a vampire. In addition, the unknown location of his remains led to the belief that his body was burned by monks to prevent him from returning from hell as one of the "undead" who feeds off the blood of the living. It is also said of the prince that in life he sealed a pact with the Devil, delivering to Satan an uncontrolled frenzy of blood and death.

Was Vlad as Cruel as the Stories Say?

One hundred years after his death, the memory of Vlad the **Impaler** still gripped the people of Europe. He reigned for only a short time, but used the most extreme violence: by some estimates, he killed or caused to be killed more than 100,000 people.

Vlad III was scornful and arrogant toward his enemies, and he used all means within his reach to maintain his power, including the most extreme violence. He had not ruled for even one year when he decided to take advantage of the movement of goods through Walachia as a source of income and declared emperor's rights (that is, the German merchants could not cross his territory with their merchandise without first offering it to the Walachian businessmen at the wholesale price). This caused the Saxon cities in Transylvania to rise against him. In retaliation, in the spring of 1457 Vlad burned and destroyed the regions of Kronstadt and Amlas. Those that did not perish in the fires were deported to Walachia and killed. Not even women and children were spared.

Wars against the Saxon cities continued for years. In 1459, Vlad imprisoned a *caravan* (a long train of people and pack animals that travel together) of 600 merchants, burned their goods, and then had all the merchants impaled. That same year,

Saxon authorities sent a committee of 55 people to Walachia to negotiate with Vlad, who received them with 55 stakes displayed in front of the palace where they were to stay. They didn't dare speak to him and returned home. Shortly thereafter, Vlad appeared in Burzenland, outside Kronstadt, where he began a true campaign of mass killing. He destroyed everything: cities, villages, and fields were leveled, and all prisoners were impaled in front of the San Jacobo church, in view of everyone. Vlad allowed himself the luxury of breakfasting among the bodies, a scene which, a century later, would be recreated in a German etching that became very popular. In 1460, Vlad's actions in Transylvania reached their maximum level of cruelty. After destroying an army that Kronstadt had sent against him and having decapitated their commander (who was first forced to dig his own grave), Vlad returned to the region and spread fires everywhere. He caused the deaths of 20,000 people. Several villages and towns remained deserted for generations thereafter.

Impalement

Impalement is an ancient method of execution. The practice differed from place to place and throughout history. However, usually in impalement, a long stake or pole with a pointed end was pushed through the human body. The other end of the stake was often forced into the ground, suspending the victim in the air until he or she was dead.

Violent Age

The terrible ferocity shown by Vlad III Dracula was nothing exceptional in a period in which executions were a popular spectacle. Mehmet II, Matthias Corvinus, and Stefan II the Great, contemporaries and neighbors, also used extreme violence when they considered it necessary. Chivalry on the battlefield was reserved only for the nobles, for whom a substantial ransom could be requested. The rest of the prisoners were wiped out. If they did not die on the battlefield or become victims of the reprisals of the victors or of the destructive fires, slavery seemed to be the easiest punishment for the inhabitants of rebel cities. Used by the sovereigns as scapegoats, the Jews, accused falsely of ungodly crimes and of carrying sickness, were subjected to purification by fire (see right) with the approval of the people. Such was the age of Vlad III Dracula.

VENGEFUL AND CRUEL

The first years of Vlad's government were also dedicated to increasing the number of his personal guards and thus reducing the influence of the **boyars.** On Easter Sunday in 1459, he invited all the boyars who until then had had some influence in the election of princes. He met with 500 of them, and he asked them how many princes they could remember. The oldest ones remembered 30, others 20, and the youngest up to eight. This was too much for Vlad, who accused them of lying and had them immediately impaled. Another version of the story is that he only impaled the old men, women, and children, condemning the young men to forced labor in constructing one of his castles, until the luxurious Easter clothes they wore fell off them in tatters. Vlad confiscated all their belongings and properties, which he then shared among his closest nobles and free peasant farmers.

Vlad III required absolute obedience. All alike had to submit to the will of the prince, since he did not agree to *primus inter pares* (first among equals), as had the old nobility in former times. Instead, his policy was *primus super omnes* (first over all), and he established a law stating that no one else could reclaim his throne.

Some people claim that Vlad was able, using methods of terror and fear, to end robbery in Walachia. To demonstrate this, he placed a pitcher of gold on a public fountain in Targoviste, which no one dared touch during his reign.

He dictated punishments without regard for class distinctions and wanted to rid his kingdom of all that he saw as "unproductive." He began with the poor, whom he invited to a feast and then burned without a thought. No one invited to the feast survived the fire. He followed with the Roma, of whom there were about 300 in the territory. He took three of them, had them roasted, and commanded the others to eat them or prepare themselves for battle against the Turks, the latter of which they all did.

Equally terrible episodes were known where the victims were monks, nobles, merchants, thieves, or beggars. No one could escape his peculiar version of "justice."

In war Vlad was equally heartless, to the point that, in 1462, he delivered a curiously detailed report to Matthias Corvinus, King of Hungary, Bohemia,

Nailed-On Turbans

After establishing his authority, Vlad III did not permit anyone to question his orders. Legend has it that when Vlad received a delegation from **Sultan** Mehmet II to require tribute, he requested that the Turkish diplomats, outfitted with their characteristic turbans, show the respect due the king and uncover their heads. The Turk spokesman responded that they never removed their turbans, not even for the sultan, and that Dracula should have known this, since he had earlier been a guest of the Ottoman court. Offended by the chancellor's response, Vlad became furious and ordered that the delegates be returned to Istanbul with their turbans nailed to their skulls so that they would never be able to remove them (a scene depicted in this painting by Theodor Aman).

and Croatia, of whom he had requested help, in which he stated: "I have killed men and women, old and young, from Pblucitza and Novoselo, where the Danube reaches the sea, to Samovit and Ghigen. We have killed 23,884 Turks and Bulgarians, without counting those whom we burned in their houses, or whose heads were not cut off by our soldiers." To reinforce his message and, since he had a detailed list of the victims in each village, Vlad III sent various bags full of ears, noses, and heads.

Toward the end of his reign, he was even able to horrify Mehmet II when he got close to the capital at Targoviste. Vlad had converted a two-mile stretch of plain into a fearful scene: 20,000 impaled Turks, Bulgarians, Germans, Hungarians, and boyars were rotting on stakes.

Making the dead stay dead

This skeleton was discovered in Poland in the 2000's. Each of the seven people buried in this grave had been executed. Their heads were then removed and placed between the legs. The ritual was to ensure that the dead stayed dead and did not rise to terrorize the living.

How and Where Did Vlad Die?

Prisoner of the King of Hungary for 12 years, Vlad Dracula regained the throne of Walachia in 1476. Most evidence indicates that he died shortly after in an ambush set by the Turks.

There is little information about the death of Vlad III, though what evidence exists seems to indicate that he was the victim of a betrayal shortly after his third occupation of the throne of Walachia in November 1476. Barely a year before, King Matthias Corvinus had freed Vlad from his long confinement when faced with the Turkish force on the borders of Hungary. According to the legends surrounding Vlad III, he and his Moldavian guard fell victim to a Turkish ambush led by a rival of Vlad for the Walachian throne, Basarab Laiota, between the years 1476 and 1477 near Bucharest in Romania. Once he was captured, according to stories at the time, his enemies cut his head to pieces.

A variation of this account states that Mehmet II hired an assassin to slip into the Walachian camp, taking advantage of the ambush in progress to decapitate the fearsome Vlad Dracula.

THE MYSTERY OF HIS GRAVE

According to tradition, the body of Vlad III was placed in the Orthodox monastery on the island at Lake Snagov, situated about 25 miles (40 kilometers) north of Bucharest. It was also believed that the body was in a tomb situated at the foot of the altar of the monastery's church, until in 1932 a team of archaeologists discovered that the coffin contained only animal remains.

That same year a second site, situated at the entrance to the convent chapel, was explored. Inside was a fragile skeleton of a decapitated man, a purple hat, a ring, a sword, a crown, and a medallion with an engraving of the Order of the Dragon.

Had Vlad III's tomb definitively been discovered? The inventory of the National Museum of Romanian History and various photographs document the tomb's contents, but the find disappeared during World War II (1939-1945). More recently, some historians believe that the objects from the tomb were buried in another location.

However, in spite of this loss, another circumstance adds to the possibility that the second tomb would contain the remains of the **Impaler.** Because Vlad Dracula gave up his Orthodox faith during his imprisonment and converted to Catholicism, it is possible that the Orthodox monks would oppose burying him under the altar on sacred ground. As an **apostate,** his body would be left at the entrance of the chapel, in a tomb that, walked on repeatedly by monks and faithful persons, would be a symbol of his eternal sorrow for having sinned against his faith.

Was His Head Sent to the Sultan?

According to the legend, after falling dead in combat, Vlad III was decapitated and his head was sent to Mehmet II inside a jar full of honey so as to preserve it. It is possible that Basarab Laiota would send it to the **sultan** for the purpose of gaining favor for himself with the powerful Ottoman ruler, who would be able to recognize the identity of the fallen **voivode**. Mehmet later ordered that Vlad's head be put on a stake and displayed for the whole world to see in the center of Istanbul. In this way, the all-powerful monarch showed the world the force of his anger and his ability to reach even the terrible impaler of the Turks.

MEHMET II

The sovereign had known Vlad Dracula in his boyhood, when Vlad was a hostage of Mehmet's father.

Vlad Tepes
Dracula

Where Do Vampires Come From?

Tales of the beings that return from the grave to feed on the living are common to nearly every culture. In Europe, records of these fearsome figures who were believed to bring death and sickness began to increase in the 1600's and 1700's.

In ancient China, classical Greece, India, among the Egyptians, the **Mongols,** the Roma, in the collection of Jewish civil and religious laws known as the Talmud. . . demons or evil spirits, including vampires, are present in all cultures. The universal nature of the myth is a response to the human desire to escape death, to achieve immortality. From this desire comes the figure of the vampire, a being connected with the demons' attempts to overturn natural and divine laws.

Two characteristics distinguish vampires the world over: they are dead people that come to life again, and, to maintain their vitality, they must drink the blood of other people. The people fed upon by vampires may sicken and die, or they may become vampires themselves. So vampires are associated with the ideas of evil spirits, of death in life, of eternal damnation, and of sickness and regeneration from human blood.

In Byzantine Europe (300's–mid-1400's), Orthodox Christianity turned the un-Christian belief in the return of the dead into a useful instrument for converting people to Christianity. Those who died after lying under oath, committing

murder, or offending religion without being sorry for their sins were said by the church to be cursed as vampires. Especially low were those who committed suicide, sinning by showing extreme pride in disregarding the divine gift of life.

The punishment also extended to those who could have been indirect victims of evil: dead bodies that were not buried with the proper last rites, children who were stillborn and had not been baptized, and it even touched on **superstition,** including bodies over which a cat jumped.

Records concerning vampires began to appear more frequently toward the end of the 1600's, and, toward the middle of the 1700's, the first books on vampirism were written. In 1746, in his work *Traité sur les apparitions,* Benedictine Augustin Calmet stated that vampires had only been known of for the past 60 years and that the references about them were found mostly in Hungary, Moravia, Silesia, and Poland.

In these areas close to the Carpathian Mountains, where Bram Stoker set the story of *Dracula,* is where the origin of the word "vampire" was first found. The term is of Magyar, or Hungarian, origin, and in the Slavic languages words similar to vampire are used to define beings

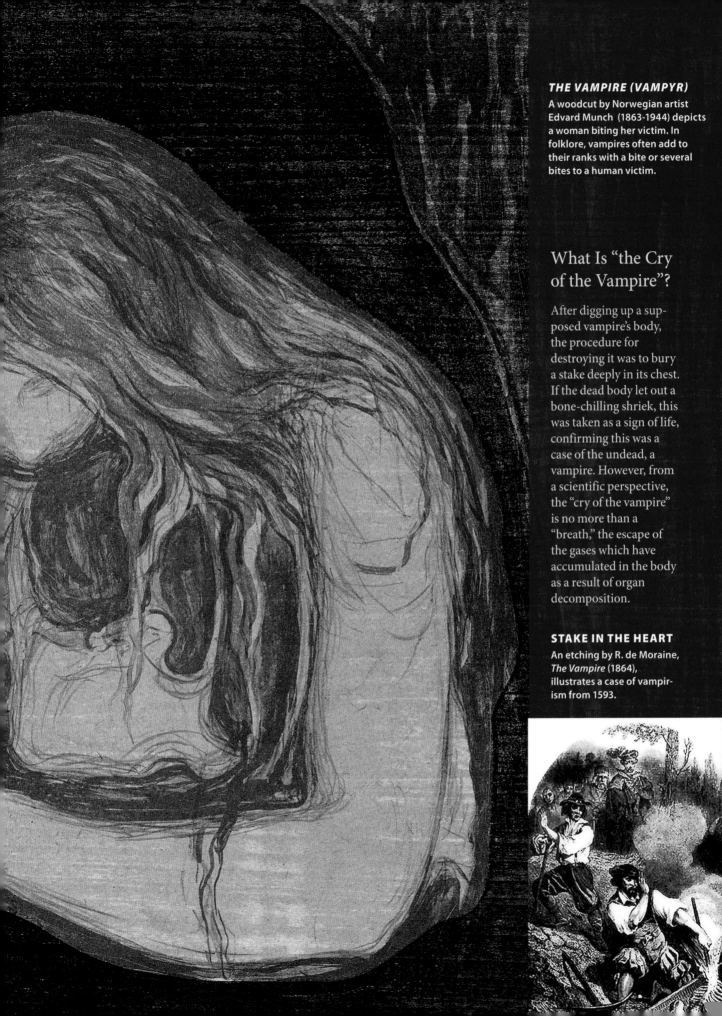

What Is "the Cry of the Vampire"?

After digging up a supposed vampire's body, the procedure for destroying it was to bury a stake deeply in its chest. If the dead body let out a bone-chilling shriek, this was taken as a sign of life, confirming this was a case of the undead, a vampire. However, from a scientific perspective, the "cry of the vampire" is no more than a "breath," the escape of the gases which have accumulated in the body as a result of organ decomposition.

STAKE IN THE HEART
An etching by R. de Moraine, *The Vampire* (1864), illustrates a case of vampirism from 1593.

PREMATURE BURIALS
This painting by Antoine Wietz, *Buried Alive* (1830), illustrates the terror of a victim of cholera being buried alive.

whose existence appears to be related to periods of widespread disease. It is no coincidence that in southeastern Europe, *epidemics* (widespread outbreaks of illness) and the idea of vampires would be connected from the end of the 1600's to the 1800's, coinciding with a succession of deadly plagues between 1708 and 1855 in Serbia, Hungary, and Poland.

VAMPIRISM AND EPIDEMICS

Today we know of the existence of germs, bacteria, and viruses, but in earlier times this knowledge had yet to be discovered. In was not unheard of for studies to be published by important universities that presented "evidence" that some symptoms of illnesses were clearly related to vampirism. In his work *Dissertatio de Vampiris Serviansibus* (1733), scholar John Heinrich Zopft gave this description: "Vampires come out at night, attack people, drink the blood from their bodies, and kill them. They indiscriminately attack men, women, and children alike, disregarding their age or sex. Those who fall under their *malignant* [evil] influence complain of *asphyxiation* [inability to breathe] and

absolute *despondency* [depression], and shortly afterward they die."

To factors such as epidemics can be added the funerary custom in southeastern Europe of burying dead bodies at a shallow depth, which would help to explain the spread of tales of vampirism in the region.

In Romania, according to Agnes Murgoci in *The Vampire in Roumania* (1926), it was customary to *exhume* (dig up) bodies after a certain length of time to see if they had become vampires. For children, this was done three years after their death, for young people after five years, and for adults after seven years. After opening the graves, people would check to see if the bodies had completely decomposed. If this was the case, they would wash the bones with water and return them to the ground. But if the body had not completely rotted away, they would pierce it with a stake or tear out the heart, which they would then burn with fire or boil. It became the usual custom to dissolve the ashes in water and give them in a drink to the sick, or use them to protect children and animals from evil. The fear of

vampires had extended so completely throughout Romania that in 1801 a bishop asked Alexander Moruzi, then prince of Walachia, to prevent the peasants from exhuming their dead.

In general terms, vampires are related to **superstitions** concerning such topics as the return of spirits; the existence of disturbed, bloodthirsty creatures; and premature burials of those in a state of *catalepsy* (people temporarily unable to move), or more permanent paralysis. (Franz Hartmann, in his work *Buried Alive* [1895], gave examples of some 700 cases of what he believed to be premature burial in the United States toward the end of the 1800's.) Other events that increased the idea of vampirism included epidemics.

According to tradition, a vampire can only be destroyed if its grave is discovered, the body is exhumed —having been found in a good state of preservation—and then nailed with a wooden stake through the heart in one blow. Augustin Calmet adds to this that it is necessary to cut off the head and tear out the heart. And for extra protection, "burn the body until it is reduced to ashes."

Porphyria, a Genetic and Hereditary Alteration of the Blood

PREVENTION

In the Middle Ages (400's-1400's), a brick was placed in the mouths of those suspected of being vampires so as to avoid spreading the plague through their bites.

Porphyria (pawr FIHR ee uh), specifically its variant Gunther's disease, has symptoms that seem similar to traits related to vampires. In the 1980's, several authors pointed this out, stating that perhaps people with this disease were the basis of the myth of the vampire. This seems unlikely. Gunther's disease is a rare genetic disorder that affects around 1 person in 1 million. It causes parts of the blood to accumulate in the skin, bones, and teeth. The disease makes the skin sensitive to light, causing it to form blisters that can break and bleed. In advanced stages, the ears, nose, eyes, or fingers might be lost to blistering and infection. The teeth might appear deep red as blood builds up in them. Given that nearly all cultures have a myth of a vampire-like creature, it is difficult to imagine that this rare disease was at the root.

PLAGUE

A German engraving from the Middle Ages of a doctor with the clothing believed at the time to protect him from plague. The beak-like mask was filled with straw and herbs to protect from "bad air." The cane permitted the physician to examine patients without touching them.

DEATH

An image from the 1500's *personifies* (shows as a person) the plague as a skeleton leaving its coffin.

Vampire Contagion

From the Middle Ages, vampires have been connected with the plague. Perhaps burial practices during the time of the plague created some of this connection. Fearing the spread of the plague, some undertakers might have prematurely buried some people seriously ill with the plague. Many plague victims were buried in large trenches in groups of many people and covered with very little soil. Some of these supposed dead persons could have abandoned or moved in their graves. This could have fed the myth of the vampire.

A World of Vampires

Stories about blood-drinking fiends, in the shape of both women and men, are among the oldest in human history. Such stories form part of the legend of the vampire.

LILITH

In Jewish legend, Lilith (in the center at right) was created by God out of the same soil as Adam. Lilith rejected Adam and became a bloodthirsty demon of the night. In this version of the story, Lilith transforms into the serpent in the Garden of Eden, tempting Adam and Eve to eat the forbidden fruit. In Jewish sacred writings, Lilith is associated with unclean animals, or monsters. Lilith and her daughter, Lilim, were thought to attack men at night and drain them of all life-giving fluids.

SEKHMET

Ancient Egyptian goddess with the head of a lioness, Sekhmet was known for her ferocity. In her angry form, she was goddess of war, slaughtering humans and drinking their blood.

An Eastern Example

Asia is no exception when it comes to tales about beings feeding off human blood. Chinese and Japanese people have their own versions of vampires. One of the most unique is the Japanese kappa, also known as the kawappa or gawappa. It is a small aquatic monster with sometimes funny and sometimes murderous habits. They are thought to kill when they have an appetite for human blood.

ITZPAPALOTL

This Zapotec statue of a bat shows Itzpapalotl, one of the Cihuateteo, the women who, after dying in childbirth, became dangerous vampire-beings according to Central American mythology.

LAMIA

Half beautiful woman, half animal, this being was feared by the ancient Greeks because she was believed to devour children. (Notice her snake skin has been shed, below, during her transformation to a human.)

KALI

This Hindu divinity is a complex figure. A benefactress and terrible being at the same time, Shiva's wife usually is seen with sharp fangs and often with a necklace of human heads around her neck. Kali may be associated with vampires because some stories claim she drank the blood of her victims in battle.

Other Vampires

Vlad Dracula is not the only royal figure to be feared as a vampire. There have been others. Among them, Hungarian aristocrat Elizabeth Báthory, known as the "Blood Countess," stands out.

Descended from a powerful family of the Hungarian aristocracy and granddaughter of a Transylvanian **voivode,** Elizabeth Báthory de Ecsed (1560-1614) became known as the "Blood Countess." Accused of witchcraft and the deaths of many girls and young women, she spent the last four years of her life captive in her castle in Cachtice, where she died.

She was thought to have kept a diary in which she recounted in great detail her terrible crimes; but her writings, like her original portrait, were lost centuries ago. She was an exceptionally educated woman for the age in which she lived: she spoke perfect Hungarian, Latin, and German in a time when most nobles were not even able to read.

The countess's story states that her bloody rituals, which would have begun around 1604, when she became a widow at 44 years of age, became sophisticated torture sessions. People claimed the countess used torture to extract the blood from the girls that she killed. She surrounded herself with a series of people who helped her in her crimes. In 1612, these servants were put on trial, judged, and condemned for witchcraft, murder, and cooperation in the disappearance of more than 30 girls and young women. They were executed.

After her death in 1614, the people prevented this "infamous woman" from being buried in sacred ground at the church in Cachtice, and her remains instead were transferred to Ecsed, in northwest Hungary, the home of her family. Based on documents from her trial, it appears the countess may have been what today we call a mass, or serial, killer. It is possible, though, that the nature and number of her crimes were exaggerated for political purposes.

ELIZABETH BÁTHORY
According to tradition, the countess described her crimes in great detail in a diary.

Gilles de Rais
(1404-1440)

Gilles de Montmorency-Laval, Baron de Rais, marshal and peer of France, devout Christian and enthusiastic follower of Joan of Arc in the Hundred Years War (1337-1453), was accused, in his later years, of being a child abuser and murderer, capable of the most terrible crimes. Around 1434 or 1435, Gilles retired from military life. He spent much of his huge fortune on a theatrical spectacle that was first performed in 1435. Gilles's family asked the pope and the king of France to stop Gilles's excesses.

Gilles was brought to trial in 1440 after he kidnapped a church official. Evidence of his apparent crimes against children was uncovered during the trial. Like Elizabeth Báthory after him, Gilles may have been a serial killer. He was found guilty of murder and was hanged on Oct. 26, 1440.

Although Gilles confessed his crimes, some scholars believe he may have been the victim of a conspiracy among high church and government officials. His figure inspired Charles Perrault, the famous writer, to create the story of Bluebeard.

Were Vlad III and the Countess Related?

Since Vlad Dracula's first wife was Cneajna Báthory, part of the powerful and noble Hungarian lineage, many believe that the "Blood Countess" was a distant relative of the Impaler. However, history and genealogy show that in spite of the coincidences, there is no blood tie between these two figures.

BÁTHORY'S TORTURES

The countess may have used systems like these coffins with nails to drain the blood of her victims.

Albert Fish
(1870-1936)

Behind his inoffensive appearance, this older American man hid his mental illness, and at 50 years of age began to murder children in New York because, he claimed, God ordered him to provide human sacrifices. Known as the "Brooklyn Vampire" and the "Gray Man," Fish tortured and murdered almost all of his victims. He also harmed himself with needles and nails. Fish was tried and found guilty of the murder of a girl and was condemned to death by electric chair in Sing Sing prison (New York).

Peter Kürten
(1883-1931)

The so-called "Dusseldorf Vampire" was born in Mülheim (Germany), into a large and poor family ruled by a violent alcoholic father. Kürten, who began his career of crime at 30 years of age in Dusseldorf, claimed that he committed his crimes to punish an unfair society. He died by the guillotine, accused of nine murders and seven attempted murders. He said he drank the blood of at least one of his victims.

Myth or reality?

According to legend, the Scotsman "Sawney" Beane and his intermarried family killed and ate many people during the 1400's or 1500's. The family lived in a large hidden cave. They hunted for victims at night. The story may have had some truth to it which was exaggerated as a tool of propaganda against Scots.

Screen Vampires

Novels about vampires gained immediate popularity, but when the blood-drinking monster became immortal on film, the myth came into its own.

Early film vampires

In the theatrical world of shadow and light, Stoker's character was destined for success. Despite notable prior attempts like *Nosferatu* in 1922, the Dracula character first debuted on the big screen in an interpretation by Hungarian actor Bela Lugosi in *Dracula* (1931), in which he played a seductive Slavic aristocrat shrouded in a broad cape. In 1958, British company Hammer Film Productions created a new image of the Transylvanian Count in *Horror of Dracula*. The vampire became more elegant and aristocratic and was surrounded by a gloomy atmosphere. The production was a success and spun off a long series of sequels over the next decade. In a more recent interpretation, Francis Ford Coppola (1939-) connected Dracula with the figure of the ruthless Vlad III in *Bram Stoker's Dracula* (1992).

FIRST FILM DRACULA
In recognition of the character that made him famous, Bela Lugosi (1882-1956), born in Transylvania, requested that he be cremated in his Dracula costume.

EARLY FILM VAMPIRE
Max Schreck (1879-1936) in a still photo from the German horror film *Nosferatu* (1922). Directed by F.W. Murnau (1888-1931), the film encountered legal problems with the estate of Bram Stoker, which refused to grant Murnau rights to the story. A judge ordered all copies of *Nosferatu* be destroyed, but, fortunately, one copy survived and was remastered.

WARRIOR PRINCE

Actor Gary Oldman (1958-) plays the medieval warrior Vlad III in Francis Ford Coppola's film version of the Dracula myth.

ARISTOCRAT

With his imposing figure and voice, British actor Christopher Lee (1922-2015) made Hammer's *Dracula* more elegant and suggestive than Lugosi's.

Vampires of love

Film versions of vampires showed them becoming less terrifying and more desirable in the 2000's. Perhaps this trend began with the television series "Buffy the Vampire Slayer" (1997-2003), which featured a human, vampire-killing teenage girl, Buffy, who was in love with at least one vampire during the series. Stephenie Meyer's "Twilight" series of books, published from 2005-2008, also featured a human teenager, Bella Swan, romantically linked with Edward Cullen, a vampire. The film adaptations of these novels appeared between 2008 and 2012.

SLAYER AND VAMPIRE

Actors Sarah Michelle Gellar (1977-) and David Boreanaz (1969-) as Buffy and the vampire Angel from the television series "Buffy the Vampire Slayer."

ROMANTIC VAMPIRE

Actors Kristin Stewart (1990-) and Robert Pattinson (1986-) star as Bella Swan and Edward Cullen in the "Twilight" series of films.

HUNYAD CASTLE

Even though it is closely associated with Vlad III, this castle, near the city of Hunedoara, belonged to John Hunyadi, Hungarian regent who eliminated the father of "the **Impaler**" and tortured his brother. However, through the years Vlad III and Hunyadi formed an alliance against the Turks.

Places to See and Visit

OTHER PLACES OF INTEREST

LAKE SNAGOV
SNAGOV, ROMANIA

Some 25 miles (40 kilometers) north of Bucharest, in Romania, lies this beautiful lake, surrounded by thick forests. In its middle is a small island, only accessible by boat, and on which an Orthodox monastery was built. Inside is the empty tomb of Vlad III, the **Impaler.** Even though today neither his coffin nor his headless body have been found, it is believed that he could have been buried in the entrance of the chapel at the monastery.

TARGOVISTE
DAMBOVITA, ROMANIA

When Vlad Dracula became the prince of Walachia for the first time (1448), Targoviste was already the capital of the principality. Situated some 50 miles (80 kilometers) from Bucharest, the city was also the scene for some of the greatest atrocities between 1452 and 1462. In Targoviste, the royal compound of the **voivodes** can still be seen, including the royal palace, the Chindia Tower, the Royal Basilica, and the Church of Saint Friday.

CASTLE POENARI
ARGES, ROMANIA

If there did exist a "true Dracula's castle," this would be the fortress built in the 1200's that Vlad Dracula occupied on a cliff above the Arges river. The then-prince chose this location because of its strategic and defensive position. Legend says that his first wife, fearful of falling into the hands of the Ottomans, committed suicide by jumping from one of its windows into the river. Vlad had to abandon the castle in 1462 when fleeing from the Turks. To arrive at the ruins of the castle, one must climb almost 1,500 steps. The views from the castle are spectacular.

Transylvania

SIGHISOARA

Founded by the Saxons of Transylvania around 1200, this city of about 30,000 inhabitants possesses one of the best preserved medieval fortresses in all of Europe, for which reason it has been declared a UNESCO World Heritage site. Inside is where Vlad III was born, and in a house in the center of the city, near where the main plaza and clock tower are located, there is a commemorative plaque to that effect on the building's front.

MUSEUM OF WEAPONS

The visit to Sighisoara would not be complete without a visit to the Museum of Weapons or the Torture Room. In the first, medieval pieces can be seen (some dating from the time of the Impaler) and in the second there are some of the torture devices from the same era.

NATIONAL MUSEUM OF HISTORY

In the most populated city in Transylvania, Cluj-Napoca–some 100 miles (160 kilometers) from Sighisoara and with the most important airport of the region– sits this museum, which provides a chronological review of the area from prehistoric times, passing through the Dacia civilization and the Roman Empire up to today. It has one of the most important collections of bronze artifacts in Europe.

Bran Castle, Brasov

Bram Stoker modeled Dracula's castle on this imposing building, although the only relationship between this palace and Vlad the Impaler was his brief attack on the palace in 1459 and being locked in one of its dungeons for two days. Located on the border between Transylvania and Walachia, this castle is an ancient Hungarian fortress from the late 1300's whose value is underlined by its singular architecture and in the collection of objects left by Queen Marie of Romania (1875-1938), whose heart also rests there. Its current owner and the authorities reject the idea that the castle is related to Stoker's character.

CASTLE OF VISEGRÁD
VISEGRÁD, HUNGARY

Visegrád, to the north of Budapest, is famous as the site of a fortress from the 1200's above the Danube. It was the summer palace of King Matthias Corvinus, one of the most important kings in Hungary during medieval times. In one of the castle's two main buildings, Vlad III was secluded for 12 years, a prisoner of the Hungarian empire. The ruins of the castle can be visited today.

CURTEA VECHE
BUCHAREST, ROMANIA

The last royal court of the Walachian voivodes, Curtea Veche, was built in Bucharest during the rule of Vlad III. Later, his brother Radu the Handsome, who had converted to Islam, was named the Pasha of Walachia by the Ottomans and lived in this residence between 1462 and 1465. Radu transferred the capital from the principality to Bucharest. Right on the side of this palace is the Old Court Church, built in 1559 and considered today as the oldest church in the Romanian capital. For two centuries, princely coronations took place in this church.

Glossary

Afterlife— Life after death.

Apostate— A person who completely forsakes, or gives up, his or her religion; a renegade or traitor.

Archaeologist— A scientist who studies the remains of past human cultures. Such remains can include buildings, artwork, and tools.

Boyar— A noble in Romania.

Dynasty— A series of rulers who belong to the same family.

Feudalism/feudal system— Having to do with a system in Europe wherein people gave military and other services to a lord in return for his protection and the use of his land.

Folklore— Beliefs, customs, and traditions among a group of people who share some connection.

Gothic— A type of fiction that became popular in England during the late 1700's and early 1800's. The plots of Gothic novels included mysterious and supernatural events intended to frighten the reader. The stories were called Gothic because most of them took place in gloomy, medieval castles built in the Gothic style of architecture.

Impale— To torture and kill someone by thrusting them upon a pointed stake. Impalement is an ancient and exceptionally cruel method of putting someone to death.

Mongol— A member of the Asiatic people now inhabiting Mongolia and nearby parts of China and Siberia. Mongols formerly lived also in eastern Europe.

Nomadic— People who move from place to place to find food, pastures for animals, or work.

Occult— Having to do with laws or forces outside of the natural world

Romanticism— A style in the fine arts and literature. It emphasizes passion rather than reason, and imagination and intuition rather than logic. It was the primary artistic style of the late 1700's to the mid-1800's.

Sultan— Ruler of the Turks (until 1922), the Ottoman Empire.

Superstition—An unreasoning fear of what is unknown, mysterious, or imaginary, especially in connection with religion.

Tribute— Money paid by one nation to another for peace or protection, in acknowledgment of submission, or because of some agreement.

Tyrant— A cruel or unjust ruler.

Voivode— Prince, in the Romanian language.

For Further Information

Books

Burgan, Michael. *Dictators and Tyrants: Stories of Ruthless Rulers*. Mankato, MN: Capstone, 2010. Print.

Indovino, Shaina Carmel. *Dracula and Beyond: Famous Vampires & Werewolves in Literature and Film*. Broomall, PA: Mason Crest, 2011. Print.

Kaplan, Arie. *Dracula: The Life of Vlad the Impaler*. New York: Rosen Central, 2012. Print.

Shone, Rob. *Vampires: Legends of the Undead*. New York: Rosen Central, 2011. Print.

Websites

"Dracula: The Metamorphosis of a Fiend." *Frontline World*. PBS, 2011. Web. 25 Feb. 2015.

Johnson, David. "The Terrifying Truth About Dracula." *Infoplease*. Pearson Education, 2007. Web. 24 Feb. 2015.

Nuwer, Rachel. "Archaeologists Think They've Found the Dungeon Where Dracula Was Kept." *Smithsonian.com*. Smithsonian, 2 Oct. 2014. Web. 25 Feb. 2015.

"Was Dracula a Real Person?" *History.com*. A&E Television Networks, 22 May 2013. Web. 25 Feb. 2015.

Index

Acknowledgments

Pictures:

© ACI

© Age Fotostock

© Alamy Images

© Album

© Bridgeman Images

© Corbis/Cordon Press

© Cordon Press

© Getty Images

© iStockphoto

© Photo SCALA, Florence

© Photo Werner Forman Archive

© Shutterstock

© Topfoto/The Image Works

The image on pg. 31: Vampire woodcut by Edvard Munch, Hamburger Kunsthalle (© Bridgeman Images)